# WOODLAND FUN AND MUD MONSTERS

## EMILY KINGTON

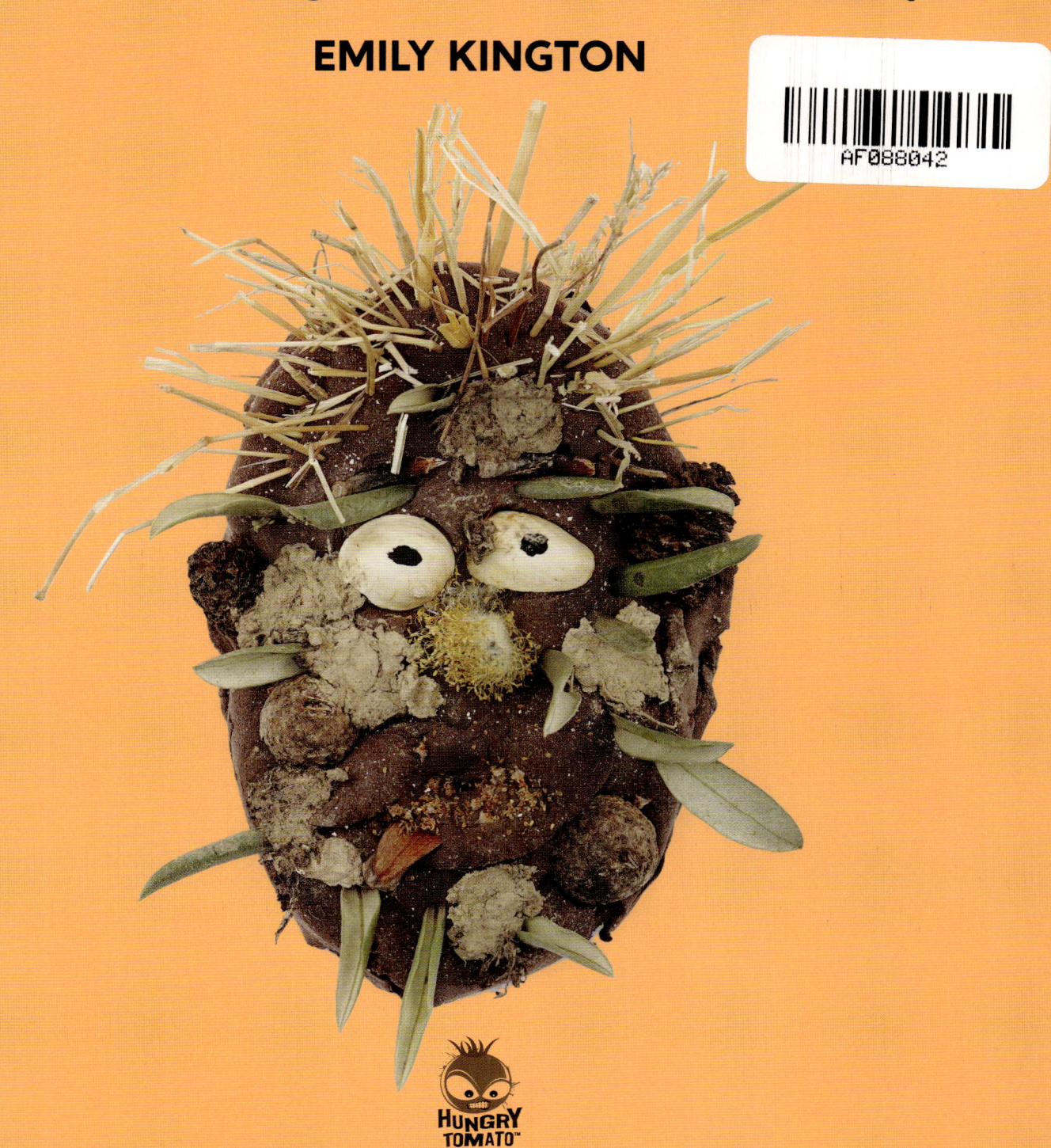

# CONTENTS

Unplug and get out into the fresh air. It's what this book is all about: exploring the outside world, trying new things, and having fun! Going for a walk is great exercise, but it can be so much more fun if you turn it into a game or use it to collect things for craft projects to make things with later.

Here are some brilliant ideas for making your outdoor adventures even more fun, plus some cool, creative projects...

**NATURE HUNT CHALLENGE** — 4

**WE ARE GOING ON A MONSTER HUNT** — 6

**SHADOW PLAY** — 8

**SHADOW PAINTING** — 9

**MUDDY MONSTER FRIENDS** — 10

**BUILD A HIDEAWAY DEN** — 12

## NEED HELP?
Watch out for this sign throughout the book. You may need help from an adult when completing these tasks.

 **MONSTER PHOTOS!**  14

 **PLANTING SEEDS** 18

 **CRAFTY PLANT POTS**  20

 **CREATIVE WOOD CRAFTS** 22

 **TAKE CARE OUT AND ABOUT** 24

# NATURE HUNT CHALLENGE

For some of these projects, you will need to take time out and go on a nature hunt!

### NATURE HUNT SAFETY

Never go out into nature alone; make sure to always go with an adult and stay together to keep safe. It can be easy to get distracted but be careful not to get separated.

Beware, some bugs can be poisonous and may bite.

Always wash your hands after handling bugs or soil.

### TAKING CARE OF THE ENVIRONMENT

Only collect nature finds from the floor. Don't pick anything off trees or plants like branches or leaves as that will damage the plant.

Treat insects with care and don't forget to release them.

### SPRIGS OF LEAVES

Leaves are great crafting materials. Look out for lots of different shapes, sizes and colours.

### STICKS

Collect sticks of all different sizes.

## STONES AND PEBBLES

Collect a mix of sizes and colours.

## MOSS

Find moss growing in woods, on fallen branches or on the forest floor. Only take a little from an area where there is already a lot.

## DECORATIONS

Dry grass, catkins, acorn tops, cones, seeds and grass bulbs.

## MUD, MARVELLOUS MUD!

Lovely sticky mud – the stickier the better. An alternative would be to use paper clay.

### YOU WILL ALSO NEED:

- Gloves
- Wellington boots
- Old bag (to carry items home)
- Small trowel/old spoon
- Pencil
- Pad of paper
- Acrylic paint
- Paintbrush
- Felt tip pen
- Craft glue
- Scissors (but don't use these without an adult)
- Plastic pots, bottles and containers
- Wooden skewer
- Hole punch
- Egg box
- Black bin bag
- Seeds
- Growing soil
- Spray bottle
- Paper towel
- String
- Water

# WE ARE GOING ON A MONSTER HUNT

Go on a monster hunt and be amazed by how the natural world is full of surprises! You can use our scoring system to rate the monsters you find or create your own.

### ON THE HUNT

On your monster hunt, take a close look at the trees and fallen branches on the ground. Take photographs of what you find and give each one a score!

## HERE IS WHAT WE FOUND ON OUR MONSTER HUNT, WHAT WILL YOU FIND?

MONSTER RATING: 3　　COOL RATING: 3　　OVERALL RATING: 6

### SCORING SYSTEM

**Monster rating**
How scary was the monster out of 5?

**Cool rating**
How cool was the monster out of 5?

**Overall rating**
Add the two scores together for a total out of 10!

Look out for eyes, noses and mouths on the trees to find your monster!

MONSTER RATING: 2　　COOL RATING: 5　　OVERALL RATING: 7

This tree looks very friendly!
Can you spot its eyes and open mouth?

MONSTER RATING: 1
COOL RATING: 4
OVERALL RATING: 5

MONSTER RATING: 3
COOL RATING: 5
OVERALL RATING: 8

This one looks strange; it almost looks like it could be some sort of animal! What do you think it looks like?

MONSTER RATING: 2
COOL RATING: 5
OVERALL RATING: 7

MONSTER RATING: 5
COOL RATING: 5
OVERALL RATING: 10

Definitely the wildest of all!

7

# SHADOW PLAY

This is one for walks on sunny days.
See what fun you can have with different shadowy shapes!

Have some fun with shadows on different surfaces.

Sometimes, you can follow your shadow... but sometimes your shadow will follow you!

When the Sun is low in the sky, we suddenly get very, very tall.

Your shadow can even be by your side.

It's not just people that have shadows; all objects and animals do, too!

## HAVE FUN WITH SHADOWS. IF YOU CAN, TAKE SOME PICTURES. THEY ARE FUN TO FRAME AND LOOK AT LATER!

# SHADOW PAINTING

You don't need to be an expert to draw, you can use the Sun to become an artist! You need to find something fun you want to draw around first of all.

## YOU WILL NEED:
- Sprigs of leaves
- Catkins
- Pencil
- Pad of paper
- Acrylic paint
- Paintbrush
- Black felt tip pen

## TOP TIP
Make sure the Sun is behind you to create a shadow.

**1.** Rest the pad against a pot and draw around the shadows in pencil.

**2.** Colour in your drawing with a black felt tip pen.

You can flick and spray paint when you're outside!

**3.** Add some sprigs of leaves and catkins for extra detail and texture.

IT'S A SIMPLE BUT EFFECTIVE WAY TO MAKE ART!

# MUDDY MONSTER FRIENDS

Make your own mud monster faces.
Take inspiration from some of these examples.

### YOU WILL NEED:

- Seeds and catkins
- Acorn tops
- Small cones
- Twigs
- Leaves
- Moss
- Mud
- Stones (big and small)
- Old plastic container
- Trowel
- Water
- Wooden skewer (to make holes and face details)

**1.** Dig up some mud and put it into an old container. You need the mud to be the consistency of wet clay - add water until it looks and feels right.

*Make a nose from extra mud.*

*Push in small stones to make teeth.*

*Push leaves or twigs into the mud for hair.*

**2.** Model the mud into the shape of a face and push it onto the trunk of a tree. Scoop out a few handfuls to make a hole that looks like a mouth!

**3.** Decorate the face with nature finds to give it features, such as eyes, eyebrows and hair! Bigger stones and moss make a great monster beard!

## USE WHATEVER YOU FIND ON YOUR NATURE HUNT. MAKE A DIFFERENT MONSTER EACH TIME!

# TINY MUDDY FRIENDS

Now you've made some huge monster faces, why not try making some smaller muddy creatures? This boggle-eyed monster is fishing. It sits perfectly on a log!

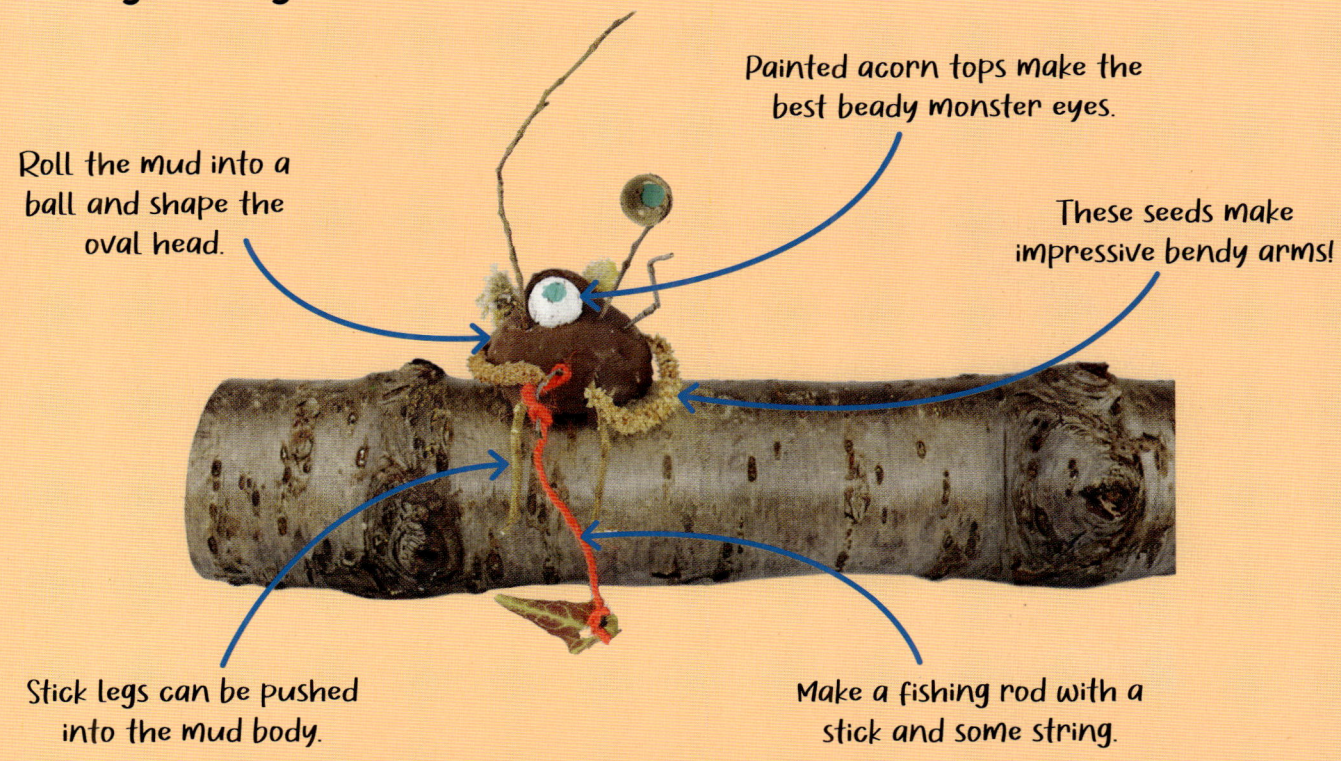

Roll the mud into a ball and shape the oval head.

Painted acorn tops make the best beady monster eyes.

These seeds make impressive bendy arms!

Stick legs can be pushed into the mud body.

Make a fishing rod with a stick and some string.

11

# BUILD A HIDEAWAY DEN

Whilst out and about on a woodland walk, make a cool camp so you can spy on small animals and birds.

### YOU WILL NEED:
- A tree with a low-hanging branch
- One really long, sturdy stick for the frame
- Big sticks and small branches
- Moss
- Leaves for camouflage

**1.** Collect all your sticks into a big pile, so that you're ready to build your den.

**2.** Lay the really long, sturdy stick over the crook of a low-hanging branch. Stack sticks on each side, all the way along, with smaller sticks at the end.

**3.** Use moss to fill in any gaps and make sure the den is sheltered.

**4.** Camouflage the outside with leaves: you don't want to be spotted!

**YOUR DEN IS READY!**
**TIME TO SIT QUIETLY AND SPOT THE ANIMALS AND BIRDS.**

# MONSTER PHOTOS!

Turn yourself and your friends into monsters with this super fun craft activity!

### YOU WILL NEED:

- Seeds
- Acorn tops
- Catkins
- Moss
- Leaves
- Flowers
- Dried flower petals
- Grass bulbs
- Cones
- Twigs and sticks
- Craft glue
- Hole punch

**1.** Choose a photograph of yourself or have one taken. Check with any adult that you can craft with your chosen photo.

**2.** Lay the nature finds over your photo to turn yourself into a scary monster. When you're happy with your design, glue the nature finds on.

# TAKE LOTS OF PHOTOS OF YOU AND YOUR FRIENDS SO YOU CAN ALL BE TURNED INTO MONSTERS!

**3.** Mount your photo onto cardboard and glue on some sticks to make a frame.

# PLANTING SEEDS

Growing your own flowers or vegetables from seed is a real achievement. Recycling pots to plant seeds in is a great way to start your own garden project!

## YOU WILL NEED:

- Seeds
- Growing soil
- Egg box (to grow seedlings in)
- Spray bottle (to water)
- Black bin bag
- Food containers or old plant pots
- Wooden skewer
- Plastic container
- Water
- Paper towel

## TOP TIP

There are different ways to sow seeds so make sure to read the instructions on the packet before starting.

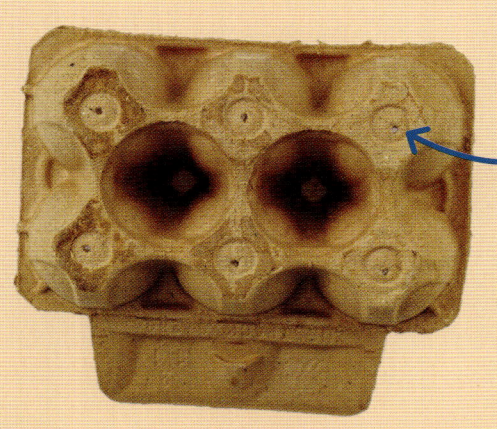

Ask an adult to make some holes in the bottom.

Seeds

**1.** Use an egg box to grow seeds into seedlings.

**2.** Fill the egg box with growing soil and put in the seeds according to the packet instructions.

**3.** Put the egg box into a container of shallow water. Allow the egg box to soak until the seeds and the top of the soil are wet.

Lift the egg box out of the water. Pour the water away and dry the container with some paper towel.

Put in a warm place and use a spray bottle to keep the soil watered.

**4.** Place the egg box back in the (now dry) container. Cover lightly with part of a black bag. Ask an adult to pierce some holes in the black bag to let some air in.

**5.** When the seeds have germinated, you can carefully transfer them into bigger pots.

## CARE FOR THEM INDOORS UNTIL THERE IS NO SIGN OF FROST, WHEN THEY CAN GO OUTSIDE.

# CRAFTY PLANT POTS

Get crafty by decorating your own plant pot for your plants to grow in!

## YOU WILL NEED:

- Coloured string
- Craft glue
- Stones (for drainage)
- Shallow dish or container
- Plants
- Pots (plastic plant pots, large yoghurt or ice cream pots, damaged planters)
- Plastic bottle or carton
- Wooden skewer
- Water

## TOP TIP

Make sure there are holes in the bottom of the pots so your plants don't get waterlogged. Ask an adult to help you make some.

Glue the end of the string to the pot to finish a colour and start a new one.

It's a bit more tricky, but you can use more than one colour at a time!

**1.** Starting at the base, wind the string once around the pot, gluing as you go. You may only need to glue the first and last layers if you keep the layers tightly wound.

**2.** Continue winding the string tightly around the pot, keeping it close to the previous layer.

## YOUR HOME-GROWN GARDEN WILL NEED TO BE WATERED REGULARLY.

# CRAFTY WATERING CAN

**In order for your plants to grow in your crafty plant pots, they need to be watered. Make this simple watering can from an old plastic bottle or carton!**

**3.** To make your own watering can, upcycle a plastic milk bottle or carton.

**4.** Ask an adult to help you make some tiny holes in the lid with a wooden skewer or similar.

**5.** Fill your bottle with water, screw on the lid and test it out!

**6.** Place some stones in the bottom of your pots, then plant your plants on top! Stand the pots in a shallow dish, and keep well-watered. The dish will stop the water escaping and running everywhere.

21

# CREATIVE WOOD CRAFTS

On a nature hunt, search for a piece of bark that you can turn into an animal and an interesting piece of wood that can be part of the sculpture.

### YOU WILL NEED:
- Interesting pieces of bark
- Nature finds like acorn tops and stones
- Spray bottle (recycle an old household spray product)
- Acrylic paint
- Paintbrush
- Plastic sheet or old cardboard or newspaper

### TOP TIP
The bark and painting in this craft is quite messy! It's best to do it outside, over sheets of old cardboard, newspaper or plastic to protect everything around you.

**1.** Keep your eyes peeled for pieces of bark - you can make them into animal shapes. This piece of bark looks a bit like a crocodile.

**2.** Look out for an interesting shaped piece of wood that you can use for a stand, in the sculpture.

**3.** The texture of bark is brilliant for a croc, but it needs a tint of green. Ask an adult to put some green paint into the spray bottle and add a tiny bit of water to thin the paint. Shake to mix and spray away!

An acorn top makes a great beady eye.

Paint on some white teeth.

**4.** Place your animal on the stand to complete the scultpure!

## WHAT ANIMALS CAN YOU MAKE FROM THE BARK AND MATERIALS THAT YOU FOUND?

# TAKE CARE OUT AND ABOUT

It's always brilliant fun when you are out exploring and gathering, but it's a good idea to take some things with you to stay safe.

### WATER
Take plenty of water. It's easy to become dehydrated in active play.

### FIRST AID KIT
Take along a basic first aid kit to deal with scratches and insect bites.

### CLOTHING
Wear appropriate clothing and footwear. It can be slippery and wet in woody areas.

## SAFETY FIRST
- Never eat any part of a plant or fungus or drink water from a stream.
- Climbing is fun and a real achievement, but check with adults before climbing anything and make sure they stay around to help you. It's not safe to climb alone.
- Beware of dangerous or poisonous wild plants and animals (applicable in some areas).
- Be careful near water. It can often be deeper than it looks.

## ALWAYS ASK AN ADULT BEFORE YOU DO ANY OF THE PROJECTS IN THIS BOOK!

Copyright © 2024 Hungry Tomato Ltd

First published in 2024 by Hungry Tomato Ltd
F15, Old Bakery Studios, Blewetts Wharf, Malpas Road, Truro, Cornwall, TR1 1QH, UK.

No part of this publication may be reproduced, stored in a retrieval system, or transmitted in any form or by any means, electronic, mechanical, photocopying, recording, or otherwise, without prior written permission of the copyright owner.

A CIP catalogue record for this book is available from the British Library.

ISBN 9781835693582

Printed in China

Discover more at www.hungrytomato.com

Picture credits:
Abbreviations: m-middle, t-top, l-left, r-right, bg-background.

Aleksey Matrenin 3bm; altanaka 8tr; Dimpank 6tl, 12tr; Emeryk III 8bm; Emily Barker 3tr; Encierro 24tr; Evgeny Atamanenko 2tl; FotoHelin 19b; Gitanna 2tm, 7tl; Hchjjl 18tr, 22tr, (warning sign used throughout); Jakub Stanek 24tm; Jasalaberry 6br; Kajasja 3tm; Lan Images 15tl; Maksimvector 9tl;Marakuliasz 8br; Nanette Grebe 3tl, 15bl; Nicky87 3bl; Remus Rigo 2tr, 8tl; Seahorse and Everest 24tl; Sergey Novikov 2br; Stig Alenas 19tr.

Every effort has been made to trace the copyright holders, and we apologise in advance for any unintentional omissions. We would be pleased to insert the appropriate acknowledgements in any subsequent edition of this publication.